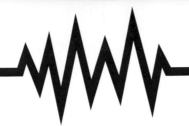

To the Rescue!™

Police Cars

Joanne Randolph

PowerKiDS press
New York

For Riley, Deming, and Hannah

Published in 2008 by The Rosen Publishing Group, Inc.
29 East 21st Street, New York, NY 10010

First Edition

Book Design: Greg Tucker
Photo Researcher: Nicole Pristash

Photo Credits: Cover, pp. 7, 9, 11, 13, 15, 19, 23, 24 (top right), 24 (bottom) Shutterstock.com; p. 5 © www.iStockphoto.com/David Lewis; p. 17 © Mario Villafuerte/Getty Images; p. 21, 24 (top left) by Jerome Pristash.

Library of Congress Cataloging-in-Publication Data

Randolph, Joanne.
  Police cars / Joanne Randolph. — 1st ed.
    p. cm. — (To the rescue!)
  Includes index.
  ISBN 978-1-4042-4153-4 (library binding)
  1. Police vehicles—Juvenile literature. I. Title.
  HV7936.V4R358 2008
  629.225—dc22

                                                2007021213

Manufactured in the United States of America

Contents

Pull over! Here comes a police car!

Police cars are there to help people in need.

Police officers drive police cars. Police officers work hard to keep us safe.

9

A police car helps out if there is trouble on the road.

A police car is used to catch people who do bad things. The police officer takes the bad person to **jail**.

13

Sometimes a different kind of police car is used to bring people to jail. This car is called the paddy wagon.

The police sometimes use dogs to help them save people or stop crime.

17

A police car has lights on top. The lights are turned on when the officer needs to get someplace quickly.

19

A police car has a radio, a computer, and more. These things help police officers do their job.

The next time you see a
police car, say thank you.
Police cars help keep us safe.

computer

jail

police officer

Index

Web Sites

Due to the changing nature of Internet links, PowerKids Press has developed an online list of Web sites related to the subject of this book. This site is updated regularly. Please use this link to access the list:
www.powerkidslinks.com/ttr/pcar/